WIND

POWER

by Kathy Allen

ENERGY LAB:
WIND POWER

CHERRY LAKE PUBLISHING • ANN ARBOR, MICHIGAN

CHERRY
LAKE
Publishing

Published in the United States of America
by Cherry Lake Publishing
Ann Arbor, Michigan
www.cherrylakepublishing.com

Printed in the United States of America
Corporate Graphics Inc.
January 2013
CLFA10

Consultants: Ryan Light, Director of Renewable Energy, Eastern Iowa College; Marla Conn, reading/literacy specialist and educational consultant

Editorial direction:
Lauren Coss

Book design and illustration:
Jake Nordby

Photo credits: Fotolia, cover, 1; Shutterstock Images, 5, 9, 13, 15, 25; Monkey Business Images/Shutterstock Images, 7; Library of Congress, 11; Photoroller/Shutterstock Images, 17; Lucas Payne/Shutterstock Images, 19; Niek Goossen/Shutterstock Images, 21; Mary Terriberry/Shutterstock Images, 23; Tom Wang/Shutterstock Images, 27

Library of Congress Cataloging-in-Publication Data
Allen, Kathy.
  Wind power / Kathy Allen.
     p. cm. – (Energy lab)
  Audience: 007-008.
  Audience: Grades K to 3.
  Includes bibliographical references and index.
  ISBN 978-1-61080-900-9 (hardback : alk. paper) – ISBN 978-1-61080-925-2 (paperback : alk. paper) – ISBN 978-1-61080-950-4 (ebook) – ISBN 978-1-61080-975-7 (hosted ebook)
  1. Wind power–Juvenile literature. 2. Wind energy conversion systems–Juvenile literature. I. Title.

  TJ820.A436 2013
  333.9'2–dc23

                              2012033414

Cherry Lake Publishing would like to acknowledge the work of The Partnership for 21st Century Skills. Please visit www.21stCenturySkills.org for more information.

TABLE OF CONTENTS

Your Mission 4

What You Know 4

Catching the Breeze 6

Dutch Windmill 9

Iowa Wind Farm 13

Wind Electricity 18

Wildlife and Wind 21

Mission Accomplished! 26

Consider This 26

Glossary 28

Learn More 29

Further Missions 30

Index 31

You are being given a mission. The facts in What You Know will help you accomplish it. Remember the clues from What You Know while you are reading the story. The clues and the story will help you answer the questions at the end of the book. Have fun on this adventure!

Your mission is to explore wind power as an energy source. Energy from wind can keep our cities and homes humming with the electricity you use every day. But how can the breeze you feel at the park turn on the lights in your house? How can it power your computer? What effects does wind energy have on the environment? Review the facts in What You Know. Then read on to learn more about the exciting world of wind energy!

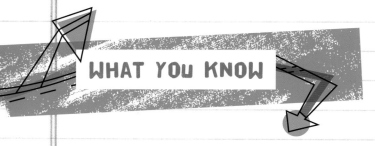

WHAT YOU KNOW

★ Today, more than 80 percent of the energy produced in the United States comes from **nonrenewable** sources such as **fossil fuels**.

★ Fossil fuels can have negative effects on the environment, and they will eventually run out.

★ Wind is a limitless, clean, and **renewable** source of power.

★ Wind farms use **turbines** to turn the power of wind into electricity.

Many people believe wind power could play an important role in the way we produce energy.

★ While the supply of wind is unlimited, the strength of wind changes.

★ Despite wind's limitations, most energy experts agree wind has an important place in our energy future.

Anthony Washington is writing a book on alternative energy sources. He's starting with wind. Follow him as he travels around the world to visit sites and interview scientists in the field. Carry out your own mission by reading his field notes.

I begin my investigation at a lake in my town. It's a warm, breezy day. Many families are out enjoying the sunshine. Sailboats stream across the lake, racing faster with each gust of wind. Children watch their kites soar high in the sky. I can see the power of the wind all around me. To get started on my wind investigation, I'm meeting with Jack Doyle. Jack is a meteorologist. He studies the earth's **atmosphere** and weather. I'm hoping he can get me started with my research by telling me a little bit about wind energy and how the wind works.

"Right now, more than 80 percent of the energy we use comes from fossil fuels," Jack begins. "Burning fossil fuels releases **carbon dioxide** and other gases into the atmosphere. Carbon dioxide traps the sun's heat. Over time, this can lead to climate change. Fossil fuels are also a limited resource. The more we use, the less we have. The less we have, the more fossil fuels cost. Right now, fossil fuels are pretty inexpensive. But as we use up our fossil fuels supply, prices will go up."

Jack explains that wind is an attractive energy source because it is completely renewable. It will never run out.

"How exactly does the wind work?" I ask.

You use the wind's energy every time you fly a kite.

Jack says wind is created by the sun heating the earth's atmosphere. When the sun heats the atmosphere, the hot air rises very quickly. Cooler air rushes in to take the place of the rising hot air. This creates wind.

Jack tells me currents of air swirl around our planet. Sometimes these currents of air are gentle breezes. Sometimes they are fierce gusts. Hills, mountains, valleys,

GREENHOUSE GASES

Burning fossil fuels releases carbon dioxide into the atmosphere. Carbon dioxide is a greenhouse gas. Greenhouse gases work a lot like a greenhouse for plants. These gases trap the sun's heat in the earth's atmosphere, making the planet warmer. Greenhouse gases help keep the earth warm enough for life. But large amounts of these gases in the atmosphere raise the planet's temperature too high. These extra gases can cause climate changes that harm the environment.

and even the earth's rotation create the gusts and breezes. This movement of air is a kind of energy called **kinetic energy**. Kinetic energy is the energy something has because of its motion. A roller coaster speeding down a hill has kinetic energy.

"Days like today are great," Jack adds. "But you've probably noticed that it's not always windy. This is a problem for wind energy. We need to find a way to capture energy from wind and store it. Then we can use wind power even when the wind isn't blowing."

As I listen, I feel the breeze against my skin. I wonder how we can use the wind to do work. ★

Today I am traveling by ferry along a set of canals outside Amsterdam, the capital city of the Netherlands. It's a beautiful autumn day. My destination appears around the next bend.

I see the wooden blades of a windmill. They are twirling just as they did 200 years ago. I've come to this

Windmills such as this one at Kinderdijk-Elshout in the Netherlands are an important part of Dutch history.

9

windmill for a tour of one of the most famous examples of wind power at work.

My tour guide, Dirk van Breda, greets me as I get off the ferry. Dirk explains that wind energy has been around for a long time. Ancient Egyptians used the wind to power sailboats on the Nile River. Ancient Persians who lived in modern-day Iran used windmills to grind grain. But that wasn't all wind power was used for.

"The Netherlands are very close to sea level," Dirk explains. He points to the windmill. "Much of our country used to be under water. In the 1400s, the Dutch used

AMERICAN WINDMILLS

Historic windmills weren't only in Europe. American farmers used windmills to pump water on the Great Plains in the 1800s. Tens of thousands of windmills dotted the landscape of rolling hills and farmland. These windmills were constructed with sturdy metal blades instead of wood. They needed to hold up under the power of the strong prairie winds. Farmers used these windmills to pump water for their livestock and crops. Many of these old mills are still in use today.

Windmills such as this one in Nebraska helped pump water for farmers to use.

windmills similar to this one to pump water away from land below sea level. They took land that was once under the ocean and turned it into valuable farmland. Let's take a closer look at the mill."

I hear a ghostly hum as we near the structure. Dirk explains that this is the sound of the turning blades. Then Dirk leads me inside the mill.

This windmill is like many of the old windmills in Europe. It has four rotating blades. The blades are set on top of a wooden tower. I look up inside the windmill. I see a horizontal bar being turned by the blades we saw outside.

"This is called the wind shaft," Dirk explains. He points out how the wind shaft turns a creaking set of gears. The gears rotate a larger upright shaft that reaches down below the floor. Gears at the bottom of the tall shaft turn a giant screw. The screw draws up water as it rotates.

"Here the kinetic wind energy outside is turned into **mechanical energy**. Mechanical energy is the energy used to do work."

It's amazing to think hundreds of years ago people created such a complicated structure that still works today. But I have more questions. How did these early windmills become the wind turbines of today? I know where my next stop needs to be. It's time to visit a modern wind farm. ★

To find out how a modern wind turbine works, I've come back home to the United States. I'm visiting Savannah Young. She's a mechanic at a wind farm in Iowa. As I get closer, I can see the wind farm from a distance. There are dozens of three-bladed turbines turning in the wind. Each turbine must be at least 80 feet (24 m) tall.

I know that wind can be noisy. But I notice another sound as I get closer to the turbines. I hear a kind of hum or

The wind rotates this turbine's three large blades, helping turn wind power into electricity.

OFFSHORE WIND FARMS

One challenge for wind farms is how much space they take up on land. But some of the most amazing modern wind farms rise directly out of the sea. Ocean winds are often stronger and faster than winds on land. This is because there are no barriers such as trees or mountains to break the wind. Offshore wind farms have groups of turbines that are often driven right into the sea floor. The Walney wind farm in the Irish Sea is one of the largest offshore wind farms in the world. It has more than 100 turbines sending electricity through cables to a station on land more than nine miles (14 km) away.

swooshing. It sounds a little like a washing machine. Savannah shouts that the blades swooping through the air create this sound. She will tell me more in a minute. It gets much quieter as we get closer to the first turbine. Savannah explains that this is because the sound of the turbine is sent outward.

"The noise is one of the reasons we try to build wind farms far away from cities and houses," Savannah says. "Still, it's not always possible to put a wind farm in the middle of nowhere. Studies have shown that the noise of a wind farm does not harm humans. But people may not want to live by them even if they don't cause physical damage."

Offshore wind farms capture strong ocean breezes without taking up any space on land.

Savannah adds, "But turbines keep getting better! Newer turbines are much quieter than older ones. Wind farms can have a few turbines or hundreds. Big wind farms similar to this one in Iowa will always take up a lot of space. The land around the turbines doesn't have to be wasted though. It can be used for grazing animals or growing crops."

I ask Savannah how this newer turbine compares with the Dutch windmill I toured. "It's the same basic idea," she says. "But there are some major differences. The windmill you saw converted wind energy into mechanical energy to run a water pump. These turbines turn wind power into electricity. It's basically the opposite of a fan you plug into the wall. Instead of using electricity to create wind, a turbine uses the wind to make electricity."

She points out the main parts of the structure we can see from the ground. "There is the giant tower, the rotor with its blades, and the nacelle. The nacelle is the horizontal casing on top of the tower," Savannah explains. "The nacelle is where the magic happens. This is where wind power is turned into electricity!" She hands me a hardhat and harness and opens the door to the tower.

"You might think strong winds are a good thing for a turbine," Savannah says. "But winds that are too strong can damage the blades. A turbine like this one has computer controls that move the pitch, or position, of the blades. Moving the blades can protect them in strong winds. Sensors at the top of the turbine measure how fast and in which direction the wind is blowing. This turbine is designed so its blades rotate in the opposite direction from the way the wind is blowing."

Savannah helps me clip my harness to safety cables. Then we climb a long set of stairs up the tower. We stop to catch our breath at several decks along the way. At the final

Wind farms around the world use many windmills to capture the wind's energy and create power.

deck, Savannah opens a steel trapdoor. I hear the very loud hum of machinery. We are inside the nacelle.

Next, Savannah opens a hatch in the nacelle. We wiggle through to stand directly on top of the giant turbine. The huge, spinning blades impress me. The scenery beyond is beautiful.

"Some people think wind farms are an eyesore," Savannah says. "And there's no doubt they change the look of the natural landscape. But I think they can be beautiful, don't you?"

I've learned a lot from Savannah and her wind turbines. But I have a couple more stops to make before I truly understand wind energy. ★

Today I am visiting an old mine pit in northeastern Minnesota. Layla Malik has offered to show me around. She is a program manager at a renewable energy research group. She keeps up on the latest developments in storing and using wind power. The former mine is filled with water. It looks like a lake. Layla says this mine could play an important role in storing wind energy.

"One of the challenges of using wind power is getting a steady supply of electricity to homes," Layla says. "Wind is not always steady. And people need different amounts of electricity at different times."

I've been wondering about this since I visited the wind farm in Iowa. "How does electricity from a wind farm get to a home?" I ask.

Layla explains that electricity from the turbines I saw in Iowa moves through something called the electrical grid. The grid is a system of wires that moves electricity from where it is created to where it is needed.

Layla says the system works pretty well, but transporting the **electric current** can be really expensive. Most wind farms are located away from residential areas.

Lakes left over from former mines, such as this one in Virginia, Minnesota, could be used to store wind energy.

This means miles and miles of wires are needed to move the power from the wind farm to a home.

"To make a long story short," she says, "we hope to use mining pits such as this one to store electricity generated by wind. Wind often blows strongest at night. We would use this extra energy to pump water from the pit uphill to a storage basin." I immediately think of the windmill I visited in the Netherlands. It did the very same thing.

Layla goes on to explain that the water would be released during the day. This is when people use more energy. The rush of water would create energy of its own.

THE ELECTRICAL GRID

What is the electrical grid? You might be able to see it right now if you look out your window. The electrical grid is a network of wires connecting towns, cities, and rural areas all across the United States and around the world. With the electrical grid all around us, it's easy to forget what amazing work it does.

Layla explains that this is a new idea that still needs testing. But batteries are another way to store electrical power.

"Think of when the power goes out in your home," she says. "An alarm clock with a battery will still work. An alarm clock plugged into the wall won't. But a battery that could store enough wind power to supply homes with electricity would need to be much, much bigger than an alarm clock battery. Some companies are testing giant batteries for this purpose."

Layla has given me a lot to think about. Every day, scientists are thinking up more ways to store wind energy. I guess wind power is a lot more than just turbines and power lines! ★

Today I'm in California meeting with Willie Davis. Willie is a researcher for an environmental group. He studies the impact of wind turbines on wildlife. His area of expertise is raptors, which are birds that hunt for their food.

Willie tells me a big concern people have about wind turbines is the threat they pose to birds and bats flying in the area. Raptors, such as hawks, are especially at risk. A hawk may not see a turbine when it is focused on hunting mice in a field.

Some people worry wind turbines could hurt or kill flying birds.

"Wind energy can be a good thing," he explains. "Turbines sometimes leak oil or other chemicals into the ground. But overall, wind is a much cleaner source of power than fossil fuels. Any energy source that does not pollute very much is a good thing for wildlife."

Willie tells me that scientists believe approximately 200,000 birds are killed by wind turbines each year. This number sounds big to me. But Willie says it is actually much smaller than the number of birds killed each year by power lines, cars, and other man-made objects. The bad news is that turbines seem to affect large birds of prey, such as eagles and hawks, more than other birds. Building wind farms away from migration routes could help cut down on bird deaths. Willie's team studies proposed wind farm sites to see if they pose a danger to birds.

Willie tells me that a well-chosen site for a wind farm would have little effect on the surrounding wildlife. I remember what Savannah told me. Cattle and other livestock can even graze beneath wind turbines! But people still have mixed opinions about building new wind farms. The Cape Wind project off the island of Nantucket in Massachusetts is one example.

"The plan to build the Cape Wind farm was controversial," Willie explains. "Local residents worried

Some species of birds migrate thousands of miles each fall and spring. These birds are especially at risk for flying into turbines.

that the farm would change the scenery. This could negatively affect tourism and property values. People also worried about the effect the wind farm would have on the environment. Those who fished for a living worried about the wind farm's effect on the fish in the area. However, some studies have shown that offshore wind farms actually provide protected areas for fish to live. Several major environmental groups spoke out in favor of the wind farm.

The wind farm could provide as much as 75 percent of Nantucket's energy needs. But residents worried their electricity costs would go up because wind farms are so expensive to build."

Wow, 75 percent sounds like a lot of energy! "How much energy do we need? Could we get all of our electricity from wind one day?" I ask.

"Maybe," Willie says. "Just 10 percent of the total wind energy on Earth is much more than the energy consumed worldwide." He tells me that the U.S. Department of Energy is studying how the United States might be able to get 20 percent of its energy from wind by the year 2030.

WIND POWER BY COUNTRY

The amount of wind energy that can be produced in a country is called its installed wind capacity. China, the United States, and Germany have the highest installed wind capacities. Other European countries actually lead the way in producing wind power. Almost 20 percent of the electricity generated in Denmark comes from wind. Portugal is close behind at 18 percent.

From what Willie has told me, wind energy may have its drawbacks. But new wind farms can be built in areas where wildlife will be in less danger from the wind farms. A lot of careful planning and research has gone into finding these sites. With scientists and engineers thinking of new ways to capture and store wind energy, there's no telling what wind energy could do in the future. ★

No energy source is perfect, but wind energy could provide a lot of energy in the near future.

Wow! You've learned a lot about wind energy. You learned that wind is a clean, renewable source of energy. In your travels, you saw how turbines can turn wind's kinetic energy into electricity. You also learned some wind energy must be stored before being sent through the electrical grid for people to use it. You saw that the cost of building wind farms and concerns for wildlife are challenges facing the wind energy industry. Finally, you learned the outlook for wind energy is bright. More of the world's electricity comes from the wind every day. Congratulations on a mission well done!

CONSIDER THIS

★ Why is wind energy a renewable source of energy?
★ How have people throughout history used the power of wind to do work?
★ How does the energy from a wind turbine reach a home or business?

★ What are some ways to store wind energy? What happens to wind energy that is not stored?

★ Which locations work best for building wind turbines?

Wind energy is already an important resource. Do you think we can find new ways to use wind power in the future?

atmosphere (AT-muhs-feer) a layer of air and gases surrounding the earth

carbon dioxide (kahr-buhn dye-AHK-side) a gas released by the burning of fossil fuels

electric current (i-LEK-trik kur-uhnt) the flow of an electrical charge through a substance

fossil fuel (FAH-suhl fyoo-uhl) coal, oil, or natural gas formed from ancient plants and animals

greenhouse gas (GREEN-hous gas) a gas that traps heat in the atmosphere

kinetic energy (ki-net-ik EN-ur-jee) the energy of motion

mechanical energy (muh-KAN-i-kuhl en-ur-jee) a type of energy that does work

nonrenewable (nahn-ri-NOO-uh-buhl) when something cannot be replaced once it is used up

renewable (ri-NOO-uh-buhl) when something can never be used up

turbine (TUR-buhn) a machine that spins an electric generator

LEARN MORE

BOOKS

Goodman, Polly. *Understanding Wind Power*. New York: Gareth Stevens Publishing, 2011.

Hirsch, Rebecca. *Motion and Forces*. Ann Arbor, MI: Cherry Lake, 2012.

Morris, Neil. *Wind Power*. Mankato, MN: Smart Apple Media, 2010.

WEB SITES

Renewable Wind

http://www.eia.gov/kids/energy.cfm?page=wind_home-basics-k.cfm

> Learn more about the wind and how we turn its power into energy.

Wind Energy Activities

http://kidsahead.com/subjects/2-wind-energy/activities

> This Web site lists experiments you can do at home to better understand wind energy.

Wind Power

http://www.alliantenergykids.com/EnergyandTheEnvironment/RenewableEnergy/022397

> Learn how a wind turbine works.

KEEP A WEATHER JOURNAL

Use the Internet or your local library to learn more about wind speeds. Then watch the weather forecast on your local news every night for one week. Keep a journal recording what the weather is like each day. How might these forecasts affect windmills in your area?

WIND FARM FIELD TRIP

Wind turbines may be closer than you think. Do you live near a wind farm? Use the Internet and your local library to research nearby turbines and wind farms. Then see if the turbines are open to the public. You might be able to sign up for a tour. If not, it's fun to just go near the wind farm to take pictures and listen to the sound of wind at work.

INDEX

atmosphere, 6-7, 8

batteries, 20
blades, 9-10, 11-12, 13-14, 16-17

Cape Wind project, 22-23
carbon dioxide, 6, 8

Dutch windmills, 9-12, 15

early American windmills, 10
electrical grid, 18, 20, 26

fossil fuels, 4, 6, 8, 22

greenhouse gases, 8

installed wind capacity, 24

kinetic energy, 8, 12, 26

mechanical energy, 12, 15
mine pits, 18

noise, 11, 13-15
nonrenewable resources, 4, 6, 8, 22

offshore wind farms, 14, 22-25

raptors, 21
renewable resources, 4, 6, 18, 26

sailboats, 6, 10

turbines, 4, 12, 13-17, 18, 20, 21-22, 26-27

wind farms, 4, 12, 13-17, 18-19, 22-25, 26
wind shafts, 12

ABOUT THE AUTHOR

Kathy Allen is a freelance writer living in Minnesota, which is part of a region known as "the Saudi Arabia of wind." She has written more than a dozen nonfiction books for children.

ABOUT THE CONSULTANTS

Ryan Light is the owner of IRIS LLC, a renewable energy design company that specializes in installing solar, wind, and microhydro technologies for remote locations all across the planet.

Marla Conn is a reading/literacy specialist and an educational consultant. Her specialized consulting work consists of assigning guided reading levels to trade books, writing and developing user guides and lesson plans, and correlating books to curriculum and national standards.